Drew's Gift of Hope

By Letina Brady Pettis

Drew's Gift of Hope
Copyright © 2025 by Letina Brady Pettis
Illustrated by: Hadia Mir.

ALL RIGHTS RESERVED. No part of this book may be reproduced in any written, electronic, recording, or photocopying without written permission of the publisher or author. The exception would be in the case of brief quotations embodied in the critical articles or reviews and pages where permission is specifically granted by the publisher or author.
LEGAL DISCLAIMER. Although the author and publisher have made every effort to ensure that the information in this book was correct at press time, the author and publisher do not assume and hereby disclaim any liability to any party for any loss, damage, or disruption caused by errors or omissions, whether such errors or omissions result from negligence, accident, or any other cause.

Published By: Pen Legacy®

Library of Congress Cataloging – in- Publication Data has been applied for.
ISBN: 979-8-218-71148-1
PRINTED IN THE UNITED STATES OF AMERICA.

DEDICATION

To my brother Drew, whose gift of hope changed lives, may this book honor you and inspire others to give the gift of life. Your selflessness and courage inspire me, and I will always carry your legacy in my heart.

AUTHOR'S NOTE:

"This story is very personal to me. After my brother Drew passed, I learned he had been an organ donor and had saved three lives. Writing "Drew's Gift of Hope" allowed me to share his legacy and the importance of organ donation. This book helps others understand the powerful impact one person can have."

Letina Brady Pettis

Tricee loved her big brother, Drew. He always looked out for her and taught her the importance of kindness and helping others.

Drew served in the military, protecting and helping others.

One day, Tricee's family received the heartbreaking news—Drew had passed away.

As her family gathered to remember Drew, Tricee overheard someone say, "Drew was an organ donor." She didn't understand what that meant.

Tricee's mother sat down with her and explained,
"Drew decided to donate his organs so he could help others.
Because of his choice, he saved three lives."

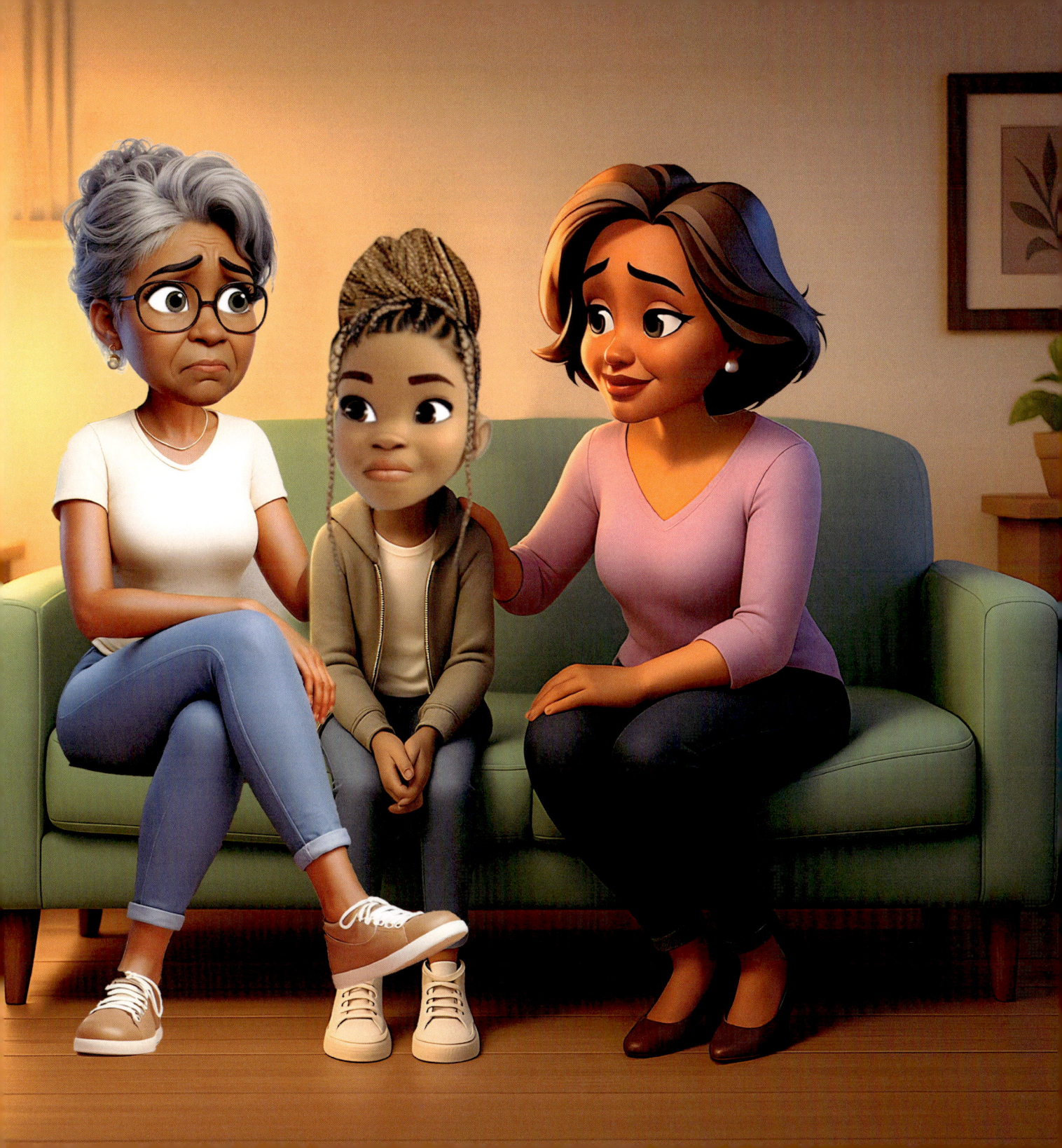

Tricee paused for a moment. "Is Drew still helping people?" she asked.

Her mom nodded. "Yes, because of Drew, three families received a second chance. His donation changed their lives forever."

Hearing this brought a smile to Tricee's face. "Drew was always ready to help others. He wanted to make a difference, even after he was gone."

She thought about Drew, from his time in the military to his everyday acts of kindness, always caring for others. Being an organ donor was just another way he made an impact.

As Tricee learned more, she wanted to share Drew's story. She told her friends, "Being an organ donor offers hope to others."

Inspired by her brother's legacy, Tricee began organizing organ donor seminars in her community, helping people understand the life-saving importance of becoming a donor.

Organ Donor Seminar

Even though she missed her brother, Tricee felt proud. "Drew's gift of hope provided others a second chance at life. His kindness will always be remembered."

Letina Brady Pettis is an award-winning author and passionate advocate. She is widely recognized for her children's books, I Want to Vote and I Voted, both recipients of the International Impact Book Award. As the founder of Get Out the Vote (GOTV) 4 Teens and the creator of National Teens Voter Registration Day, Letina is committed to empowering young voices and promoting civic engagement. Through her book Drew's Gift of Hope, she honors her brother's legacy and raises awareness about the life-saving impact of organ donation.

www.ingramcontent.com/pod-product-compliance
Lightning Source LLC
LaVergne TN
LVRC091354060526
838201LV00042B/418